Our Journey to Christmas with Pope Francis

Rev. Nick Donnelly

Dedicated to my much loved Aunty Pat,
who has inspired and encouraged me
in my discipleship of our Lord

*All booklets are published thanks to the
generous support of the members of the
Catholic Truth Society*

CATHOLIC TRUTH SOCIETY
PUBLISHERS TO THE HOLY SEE

Contents

ISBN 978 1 78469 138 7

FIRST WEEK OF ADVENT
Advent is a journey to meet God

Prayers for the First Week of Advent

Grant your faithful, we pray, almighty God,
the resolve to run forth to meet your Christ
with righteous deeds at his coming

Collect for the First Sunday of Advent

May these mysteries, O Lord,
in which we have participated,
profit us, we pray,
for even now, as we walk amid passing things
you teach us by them to love the things of heaven
and hold fast to what endures.
Prayer after Communion for the First Week of Advent

Intention for the First Week of Advent

During the First Week of Advent, Pope Francis invites us to set out with him on the journey to meet God. The Holy Father wants each one of us to "resolve to run to meet your Christ" and be awake to the truth that we "walk amid passing things" towards the "things of heaven" that endure.

Our journey to meet God

Pope Francis sees Advent and Christmas as a journey, in fact as two journeys: our journey towards God and God's journey towards us. The Holy Father wants us to understand the nature of our journey towards Christmas so we don't get sidetracked or lost on the way. He also wants to help us cultivate the right dispositions necessary to undertake this Advent journey. If we follow his advice in our day-to-day lives during this season, we will place ourselves in the right place for God to meet us in his journey from heaven to earth. This is how Pope Francis puts it:

> The season of Advent is a time when the Church and the People of God journey anew toward Christmas; we journey to an encounter with the Lord. Christmas is not merely a commemoration in time nor simply a memory of something beautiful. Christmas is something more. We travel down this path to meet the Lord. During the season of Advent, then, we journey to meet him, to encounter him with our hearts and our lives, to meet him, the living One, as he is; to meet him in faith.[1]

We so often hear the Christian life described as a "journey" that it has become a commonplace expression that we pass over with the casual assumption that we know what is meant by the metaphor. However, during this season of Advent and Christmas, Pope Francis wants each one of us fully to know and live this wonderful, miraculous journey we call the Christian life.

Journeys to meet God

Journeys to meet God are a fundamental experience and reality of the Bible - Abraham's journey to the Promised Land where he met the Lord in the firebrand of the Covenant; Moses and the Hebrew tribes journey from slavery to Mount Sinai where they met the Lord, YHWH, in the cloud of glory; Elijah's journey to Mount Horeb where he met the Lord in the sound of silence after the storm.

These Old Testament journeys to meet God culminate in, and are transcended by, Our Lady's and St Joseph's journey to Bethlehem, and the journeys of the poor shepherds and the Wise Kings in homage of God become man. Here the mystery of God coming to his people is revealed in the littleness of the baby Jesus.

All these journeys attain their fulfilment and completion in the ultimate journey of man's encounter with God. This is Our Lord's journey from Galilee to Jerusalem where the mystery of God is fully revealed in the vulnerability of Christ – true God, true man – hanging on the Cross of Golgotha. Here all journeys cease; God and man are reconciled. This is the journey we are now caught up in - the Church's journey towards that consummation of this reconciliation when the heavenly Jerusalem descends to earth, and the Bridegroom comes to welcome his Bride to the Wedding Feast of the Lamb at the end of time.

Pope Francis's guide to the journey

In light of this, it is understandable why the image and language of "journey" is one of Pope Francis's favourite ways of describing the Christian life. In his first homily as pontiff, the very first image he used was that of a journey:

> Journeying. "O house of Jacob, come, let us walk in the light of the Lord" (*Is* 2:5). This is the first thing that God said to Abraham: walk in my presence and live blamelessly. Journeying: our life is a journey, and when we stop moving, things go wrong. Always journeying, in the presence of the Lord, in the light of the Lord, seeking to live with the blamelessness that God asked of Abraham in his promise.[2]

Pope Francis has provided us with a map of the journey, pointing out that its essential direction is both outward and inward: out towards others and in towards our heart where God awaits us. "This dual journey is the double path that Jesus wants from his disciples."

The outward journey Jesus wants from us is to go out in service of others, through corporal and spiritual acts of mercy. Jesus sends us out "to proclaim the gospel, to go out to bring salvation, the gospel of salvation" and to "serve others". Going out to others in service is so essential to the Christian life that if we don't do this we can't call ourselves Christian:

If a disciple does not walk in order to serve, his walking is of no use. If his life is not for service, his life is of no use, as a Christian. [One can become boastful and say], "Yes, I am a Christian; I am at peace, I confess, I go to Mass, I follow the commandments." But where is the service to Jesus in the sick, in the imprisoned, in the hungry, in the naked? This is precisely what Jesus told us we must do because he is there…service to Christ in others.[3]

The inner journey, according to Pope Francis, is just as important to the Christian life as the outward journey because without it the gospel that we take "to others will be weak, watered down - a gospel with no strength":

But there is another path of the disciple of Jesus: the inner journey, of the disciple who seeks the Lord every day, through prayer, in meditation.[4]

Choosing to make the journey

Undertaking this journey doesn't happen automatically just because we call ourselves Christians. It requires our decision and commitment, not only to set out on the journey, but also to persevere and stay the course, co-operating with the grace and providence of God. As the *Catechism of the Catholic Church* expresses it:

Angels and men, as intelligent and free creatures, have to journey toward their ultimate destinies by their free choice and preferential love. They can therefore go astray. Indeed, they have sinned. (*CCC* 311).

Pope Francis, as an experienced guide to the spiritual life, cautions us about the missteps and pitfalls that face us on our journey. He advises us to orientate ourselves correctly on the journey with this passage from the Gospel of John:

> "And after I have gone and prepared you a place, I shall return to take you with me; so that where I am you may be too. You know the way to the place where I am going." Thomas said to him, "Lord, we do not know where you are going, so how can we know the way?" Jesus said, "I am the Way, the Truth, and the Life. No one can come to the Father, except through me." (*Jn* 14: 3-6).

The fundamental truth that Pope Francis wants us to draw from Our Lord describing himself as "the Way" is to realise that to be a genuine Christian we must be constantly moving forward on the Way of Christ, "with Baptism we begin to walk, and walk and walk". By this the Holy Father is referring to our vocation to holiness, which is to become more and more like Our Lord. As the Second Vatican Council puts it, we "must follow in his footsteps and conform [our]selves to his image seeking the will of the Father in all things." (*Lumen Gentium*, 40).

Walk in love, as Christ loved us

In Catholic spiritual life, this following ever closer in Our Lord's footsteps into holiness is called the *imitatio Christi*, the imitation of Christ. The apostles describe the whole Christian life as an ever closer imitation of Christ:

> This, in fact, is what you were called to do, because Christ suffered for you and left an example for you to follow the way he took. (*1 P* 2:21) Try, then, to imitate God, as children of his that he loves, and follow Christ by loving as he loved you, giving himself up in our place as a fragrant offering and a sacrifice to God. (*Ep* 5:1).

Thomas à Kempis's devotional book, *The Imitation of Christ*, used to be, after the Bible, the most widely read book of Christianity, but the phrase "imitation of Christ" has become less popular in our time. This might be due to the association of the word "imitation" with forgery and fakes. This is unfortunate because truly living in imitation of Christ means leaving behind the fakery and falseness of sin for the authentic holiness of Christ. A true understanding of the *imitatio Christi* will help us, through deepening our knowledge of Christ and by co-operating with his grace, to become more and more like him in our attitudes and behaviour. By so doing, we will live our lives out of the truth that Our Lord is the Way, the Truth and the Life. As Thomas à Kempis put it:

> Follow Me. I am the Way, the Truth, and the Life. Without the Way, there is no going. Without the Truth, there is no knowing. Without the Life, there is no living. I am the Way which you must follow, the Truth which you must believe, the Life for which you must hope. I am the inviolable Way, the infallible Truth, the unending Life. I am the Way that is straight, the supreme Truth, the Life that is true, the blessed, the uncreated Life. If you abide in My Way you shall know the Truth, and the Truth shall make you free, and you shall attain life everlasting. (*The Imitation of Christ, chapter 56*).

Again and again Pope Francis encourages us to imitate Jesus, to love like Jesus, to serve others like Jesus, to be merciful and forgiving like Jesus. When we put the needs of others before our own needs we truly imitate Our Lord, who "came not to be served but to serve, and to give his life as a ransom for many." (*Mt* 20:28):

> Serving and giving oneself for others may make one seem like a loser in the eyes of the world, but in reality that person is imitating Christ's love and service, which conquered death and gave life to the world.[5]

The four ways we can get lost

Pope Francis identifies four ways in which we can get ourselves lost by failing to follow Jesus as the Way, the Truth and the Life:

Spiritual mummies. These are Christians who stop growing in their spiritual lives, who are lukewarm disciples, "neither cold nor hot". (*Rv* 3:15) They follow the external observances of being Christian, going to Mass, praying devotions, contributing to the needs of the Church, but their hearts remain hard and unmerciful towards others:

> A Christian who doesn't walk, who doesn't make his way, is an "unChristian" Christian, so to speak: he is a somewhat pagan Christian, standing there, standing still, immobile, he does not go forward in Christian life. He does not bring the Beatitudes to fruition in his life. He does not do works of mercy. He stands still. Pardon the word, but it is as if he were a "mummy", there, a "spiritual mummy". Indeed, there are Christians who are "spiritual mummies", standing still, they don't do anything bad, but they don't do anything good. However, this way of being does not bear fruit: they are not fruitful Christians because they do not walk.[6]

Stubbornly lost. Every Christian loses his way on the journey. We all fall into sin and lose track of the right way to go. But there are those Christians who stay lost because, even though they realise they've taken the wrong path, they refuse to admit their sin, and thereby fail to hear Our Lord calling them back onto the right path:

> There are some who walk and go astray as we too, often go astray. It is the Lord himself who comes and helps us. It is not a tragedy to go astray. In fact, the tragedy is being stubborn and saying: "this is the way", and not letting the Lord's voice tell us, "This is not the way, turn around and go the right way". It is important to go back to the right path when we realise our errors, the mistakes we make and not to be stubborn and always go astray, because this distances us from Jesus, because he is the Way.[7]

The traditional word for admitting that we're lost and turning round to follow the Lord's voice is "conversion". We know our journey is going in the right direction when we accept that it consists of a series of conversions as we grow in knowledge of our own sinfulness and our need for Our Lord's help. The stubborn reject the need for conversion.

Misguided wanderers. This type of Christian is forever restless, always seeking something novel, such as new way of praying or a different parish or a new theology that breaks with the "old" doctrines of the Church or even a new religion that mixes together various elements from different world religions:

> There are others who walk but don't know where they are going: they are misguided in Christian life, wanderers. Their life amounts to roaming, here and there, thus losing the beauty of drawing near to Jesus in life. In short, they lose their way because they roam and so often this roaming, this misguided wandering, leads them to a life with no way out: too much wandering transforms life into a labyrinth and then they don't know how to get out. Thus, in the end, they have missed Jesus's call, they have no compass to find the way out and they wander, they roam, they search.

Mesmerised to a standstill. This type of Christian gets fixated on one aspect of Christian life to the exclusion of all else, such as a way of celebrating Mass or an issue of social justice or a place of pilgrimage or a particular parish. Such aspects of Christian life may be good in themselves, but they become harmful when they become the sole focus because they make a person feel peaceful and secure in a restless, insecure world. There is always the danger of any created thing becoming an idol that stops us truly following in the footsteps of Our Lord:

> There are others on the journey who are seduced by beauty, by something, and they stop midway, mesmerised by what they see, by that idea, by that proposal, by that landscape, and they stop. But Christian life is not charm, it is truth. It is Jesus Christ. And St Teresa of Avila said, speaking about this journey: "We are walking in order to arrive at the encounter with Jesus"…Indeed, Christian life must continue. It is important to ensure that something beautiful, something peaceful, a peaceful life does not mesmerise me so as to stop me.[8]

Pope Francis's examination of conscience for the journey

Pope Francis recommends that we frequently undertake an examination of conscience in order to check if we're following the Way of Jesus or have gone astray. The Holy Father insists that we often take "five short minutes" to take our bearings on the journey. He recommends the following questions:

- How is my Christian journey, which I began in Baptism?

- Am I standing still? Have I gone astray? Am I constantly wandering, not knowing where to go spiritually?

- Do I stop at things that I like: worldliness, vanity - so many things?

- Do I always go forward, making the Beatitudes and the works of mercy tangible?

- How am I walking? Am I following Jesus? Is he the Way I am following?

- "Let us ask the Holy Spirit to teach us to walk correctly, always, and when we get tired, let us take a short rest and go on. Let us ask the Lord for this grace."[9]

Journey to the Mountain of the Lord

At the beginning of Advent, Pope Francis wants us to set out on our journey towards Christmas with deeper awareness of the nature of the Christian life as a journey. He also wants us to take our bearings to make sure we're going in the right direction, and that we have the right attitudes to see us through to our final destination - the adoration of the baby of Bethlehem and the adoration of the Lamb in Heaven.

The sacred Scriptures of Advent are essential "way posts" that point us on the right direction to take during the four weeks. Pope Francis's first Advent homily as pope was on the Book of the Prophet Isaiah:

It shall come to pass in the latter days
that the mountain of the house of the Lord
shall be established as the highest of the mountains,

and shall be raised above the hills;
and all the nations shall flow to it,
and many peoples shall come, and say:
"Come, let us go up to the mountain of the Lord,
to the house of the God of Jacob;
that he may teach us his ways
and that we may walk in his paths."
(*Is* 2:1-3)

The Holy Father wants us to learn two essential truths from Isaiah's image of journeying to the mountain of the Lord: always remember that your life is a journey with a purpose, and make the goal of your life meeting Jesus.

*Always remember that your life is a journey
with a purpose*

In the First Reading we heard the Prophet Isaiah speak to us about a journey, and he says that in the latter days, at the end of the journey, the mountain of the Lord's Temple shall be established as the highest mountain. He says this to tell us that our life is a journey: we must go on this journey to arrive at the mountain of the Lord, to encounter Jesus.[10]

All around us we see people who have lost their way because they have forgotten, or rejected, the truth that our lives are a journey towards the mountain of the Lord. Our culture is sinking in world-weary cynicism, hopelessness and violence because people are not journeying towards God. The image of the "mountain of the Lord" means that we journey in the expectation of finding God in this world, not only in heaven. A mountain is the biggest, the most solid, object on the planet. It indicates that the destination of our journey is not some dreamlike, far off utopia, it is an encounter with God that will be unmistakable and very real.

Make the goal of your life meeting Jesus

We must go on this journey to arrive at the mountain of the Lord, to encounter Jesus. The most important thing that can happen to a person is to meet Jesus: this encounter with Jesus who loves us, who has saved us, who has given his life for us. Encounter Jesus. And we are journeying in order to meet Jesus.[11]

One of the wonderful things about Advent is that it recapitulates the purpose of our lives: a journey to meet the Lord. The expectation and preparation we experience in the four weeks leading up to Christmas enable us to get back in touch with the expectation and preparation that are the hallmarks of a Christian life orientated towards its true purpose - to meet God.

A Prayer for the First Week of Advent

Lord, we ask for the grace to make this journey with several dispositions that will aid us. Perseverance in prayer: to pray more. Diligence in fraternal charity: to draw closer to those in need. And joy in praising you, Lord. May we begin this journey in prayer, charity and praise, so that you, Lord, might come to meet us. May we allow you to meet us with our defences down, in openness. Amen.[12]

Reflections: My journey to meet God

Do I see my life as a journey?

Am I journeying

- Inwards towards God, and,
- Outwards towards others in love?

Do I journey in, and because of, the grace of faith, cherishing this gift?

Look again at Pope Francis's examination of conscience:

- How is my Christian journey, which I began in Baptism?
- Am I standing still? Have I gone astray? Am I constantly wandering, not knowing where to go spiritually?

- Do I stop at things that I like: worldliness, vanity - so many things?

- Do I always go forward, making the Beatitudes and the works of mercy tangible?

- How am I walking? Am I following Jesus? Is he the Way I am following?

Ask the Holy Spirit for grace to walk correctly in prayer, charity and praise, imitating Our Lord.

Second Week of Advent

Enter into the mystery of salvation

Prayers for the Second Week of Advent

Almighty and merciful God,
may no earthly undertaking hinder those
who set out in haste to meet your Son,
but may our learning of heavenly wisdom
gain us admittance to his company.

Collect for the Second Sunday of Advent

O God, who have shown forth your salvation
to all the ends of the earth,
grant, we pray,
that we may look forward in joy
to the glorious Nativity of Christ.

Collect for Tuesday, Second Week of Advent

Intention for the Second Week of Advent

During the Second Week of Advent Pope Francis guides us along the path of the greatest event in history - God's saving journey with mankind from the Garden of Eden to the Garden Tomb of the Resurrection. The Holy Father wants each one of us to be filled with thankful joy to God,

22

"who has shown forth" his "salvation to all the ends of the earth", and thereby we may learn "heavenly wisdom" that gains "us admittance to his company".

The journey of salvation history

Above all else, Advent is the time when the Church, and we ourselves, prepare to celebrate fittingly and worthily one of the greatest divine mysteries and the greatest event in human history: the Incarnation of the Son of God. The conception and birth of Jesus at Bethlehem are the beginning of the definitive fulfilment of the history of God's saving acts that can be traced back to the Garden of Eden and which culminate in Our Lord's Resurrection from the garden tomb close by Golgotha in Jerusalem.

Pope Francis has a passion for salvation history, and he wants to share his passion with us during Advent. He knows it will change the way we see human history and will transform the way we live our own personal salvation histories. The Holy Father sees salvation history as the heart of the Christian faith:

Our faith is not only centred on a book [Sacred Scripture] but on a history of salvation and above all on a Person, Jesus Christ, the Word of God made flesh. Precisely because the horizon of the divine word embraces and extends beyond Scripture, to understand it adequately the constant presence of the Holy Spirit is necessary, who "will guide you into all truth" (*Jn* 16:13).[13]

What is salvation history?

Pope Francis thinks it's important that during Advent we
know what the Church means by salvation history. The
Catechism of the Catholic Church calls God's plan of
salvation the history of salvation, and explains that it is the
unique history of the Most Holy Trinity's loving initiatives
for the sake of humanity:

> The whole history of salvation is identical with the
> history of the way and the means by which the one true
> God, Father, Son and Holy Spirit, reveals himself to
> men "and reconciles and unites with himself those who
> turn away from sin". (*CCC* 234).

The New Testament uses a special phrase to explain the
Holy Trinity's loving plan of salvation: the mystery of
God. "Mystery" is not used in the modern sense of the
word meaning a puzzle to be solved or unusual events
that at first are difficult to understand, but become clearer
with the discovery of evidence. St Paul writes about God's
hidden plan of salvation that has been fully revealed in
Jesus Christ:

> The message which was a mystery hidden for
> generations and centuries has now been revealed to his
> saints…The mystery is Christ among you, your hope of
> glory. (*Col* 1:26;27).

> For he has made known to us in all wisdom and insight the mystery of his will, according to his purpose which he set forth in Christ as a plan for the fulness of time, to unite all things in him, things in heaven and things on earth. (*Ep* 1:9-10).

The Church continues to use the word "mystery" to refer to Jesus Christ as the revelation of God's hidden plan of loving goodness. Jesus Christ is the definitive expression of the mystery of God, revealing the invisible God in the flesh. He manifests the saving plan of God because he is, in his own person, the presence of God, and his deeds are the fulfilment of that plan. Salvation history is not dead history because the Risen Christ is the fulfilment and living revelation of God's plan of salvation. Therefore, we can participate in the realities of salvation history in the here and now through faith and the sacraments of the Church. Our participation in the mysteries of Jesus Christ is the whole purpose of the Incarnation, so that we would come to share the divine nature.

Pope Francis knows that, as it is the feast of the Incarnation, there can be no better time than Advent and Christmas to immerse ourselves through faith and the sacraments in salvation history.

Christmas is not a myth; Christmas is history

It is common during Advent and Christmas for secularists to accuse us of celebrating a "myth". Pope Francis wants us to be clear that during Advent and Christmas we are celebrating real, historical events: "salvation is always in history: there is no salvation without history";[14] "Our salvation, the one God wanted for us, is not an aseptic, manufactured salvation, but historical".[15] By stressing that we are saved by God intervening through real historical events, Pope Francis is continuing an emphasis of Pope Benedict XVI's teaching:

> It is of the very essence of biblical faith to be about real historical events. It does not tell stories symbolising suprahistorical truths but is based on history, history that took place here on earth...*Et incarnatus est* [*He became incarnate*] - when we say these words, we acknowledge God's actual entry into real history. (Pope Benedict XVI, *Jesus of Nazareth*, vol.1, p.xv).

Why did God become a vulnerable, powerless baby?

One of the profoundest questions facing man is why did God become man? Why did the almighty, uncreated God become incarnate as a vulnerable, powerless baby? Pope Francis's simple answer is that God did not want to be distant, but wanted to come close to human beings.

Pope Francis sees the genealogy of Jesus in the Gospel of Matthew, 1:1-17, as conveying the truth that God wants to journey with human beings:

> …and Jacob was the father of Joseph the husband of Mary; of her was born Jesus, who is called Christ. The sum of generations is therefore: fourteen from Abraham to David; fourteen from David to the Babylonian deportation; and fourteen from the Babylonian deportation to Christ . (*Mt* 1:16-17).

Taking the dry genealogical list from St Matthew, the Holy Father draws the following conclusions about the "heavenly wisdom" that planned the Incarnation of the Son of God.

Consubstantial with the Father and with Mary

Pope Francis believes that the word "consubstantial" conveys the mystery of God wanting to become close to us. We say the word "consubstantial" every time we pray the Nicene Creed:

> I believe in one Lord Jesus Christ,
> the Only Begotten Son of God,
> born of the Father before all ages.
> God from God, Light from Light,
> true God from true God,
> begotten, not made, consubstantial with the Father.

According to the *Catechism*, "consubstantial" means "one in being", so the Son of God is one in being with God the Father and God the Holy Spirit. Furthermore, the *Catechism* explains that, according to the Council of Chalcedon, the Son of God is consubstantial with us: one in being with us in terms of his humanity. This means that God and man are united in Our Lord Jesus Christ at the level of being. God's desire to be close to man was so strong that he united himself to us in this mysterious way. As the Second Vatican Council puts it, "For by his Incarnation the Son of God has united himself in some fashion with every man." (*Gaudium et Spes* 22).

This is how Pope Francis explains our close union with God, referring to the genealogy of Jesus in Matthew:

> We are not dealing with a list in a telephone book, but with pure history…God sent his Son among men. Jesus is consubstantial with God, the Father, but also consubstantial with his mother, a woman. And this is his consubstantiality with his mother: God entered history, God wanted to become history. He is with us. He has journeyed with us".[16]

The Immaculate Conception of the Blessed Virgin Mary

During Advent we celebrate the Immaculate Conception of Mary, on the 8th of December, which takes us into the heart of the mystery of Jesus being consubstantial with his mother. Pope Francis sees the Immaculate Conception of Mary as a great act of God's mercy, an essential moment in his plan of salvation history.

The phrase *"Hail, full of grace, the Lord is with you"* (*Lk* 1:28) is unique in Scripture, with nothing similar found in the other annunciations of births. The Archangel Gabriel's declaration "Hail, full of grace" gives Mary a special status among humanity, implying that she has been chosen to play a unique role in God's plan. Mary is the unique object of God's grace because of her appointed role as the Mother of God. This greeting by the angel, rather than her proper name, defines who Mary is. It defines who Mary is for God.

In harmony with the requirement for Mary to submit herself completely to the will of God, God chooses that Mary receives grace throughout her life, that is, from the moment of her conception when she was conceived immaculate, without original sin. It is important to note that Mary's receipt of the fulness of grace, and the unique holiness she receives is "by reason of the merits of her Son". (*CCC* 491) She is not divine or a parallel Saviour. Though Mary receives unique graces to fulfil her unique role in salvation history, she remains a human being. The immaculate conception of Mary serves to emphasis the fact that Jesus is truly human and without sin. Mary contributes the "essential" human element from the race of Adam, but free from sin. She is enabled by the grace of God physically to overcome her human limitations and give birth to Christ who is the New Adam: "*Mary is thus enabled to do what, outside of this grace, no human creature ever could, Mother into being the very person of the Incarnate Son*". (*Jacques Servais*)[17]

Pope Francis explains the significance of the immaculate conception of Mary in God's plan of mercy and forgiveness of our sins. For the Holy Father, the Immaculate Conception is not some remote event of history, but an ever present reality that touches the life of each one of us.

The feast of the Immaculate Conception expresses the grandeur of God's love. Not only does he forgive sin, but in Mary he even averts the original sin present in every man and woman who comes into this world. This is *the love of God which precedes, anticipates and saves*…The history of sin can only be understood in the light of God's love and forgiveness…Were sin the only thing that mattered, we would be the most desperate of creatures. But the promised triumph of Christ's love enfolds everything in the Father's mercy. The word of God which we have just heard leaves no doubt about this. The Immaculate Virgin stands before us as a privileged witness of this promise and its fulfilment.[18]

God enters man's history of sin and holiness

Pope Francis also concludes from Our Lord's genealogy that God loves us so much that he wants to be close to us, to be united with us, even though we are sinners. Salvation history shows us that God does not reject sinful humanity or individual sinners, but allows his revelation, the pure and holy self-communication of his inner life and grace, to be held in weak, fragile vessels, human beings. In his mercy, he chooses to associate with habitual sinners. Our history is one of repeat offending! We don't deserve it, we've done nothing to merit it, but because he loves us so much God chooses again and again as the vessels of his holiness "the dirty hands of men". The holiness of Christ radiates from the midst of man's sin. The Holy Father explains it this way:

> It is a history wrought of holiness and sin. The list of the genealogy of Jesus is filled with saints and sinners: from Abraham and David who converted after his sin to high calibre sinners, who sinned gravely. But God made history with them all. The latter were sinners who did not know how to respond to the design God had in mind for them. Solomon, so great and intelligent, ended like a poor man who didn't even know his name. And yet God was also with him. And this is beautiful: God makes history with us.[19]

Jesus is the Incarnation of the Father's mercy

When Pope Francis writes that "Jesus Christ is the face of the Father's mercy" he is taking us deeper into the mystery of the Incarnation. The Holy Father describes Jesus as "mercy incarnate", [20] an insight he acknowledges as originating with Pope Benedict XVI. In 2008 Pope Benedict XVI said during a Regina Cæli address on Divine Mercy Sunday:

> Indeed, mercy is the central nucleus of the Gospel message; it is the very name of God, the Face with which he revealed himself in the Old Covenant and fully in Jesus Christ, the Incarnation of creative and redemptive Love. May this merciful love also shine on the face of the Church and show itself through the sacraments.[21]

The face is the most intimate expression of the person, communicating thoughts and emotions. The understanding of Jesus as the face of the Father conveys the reality of God wanting to get close to human beings.

Pope Francis even describes the intimacy between Mary and baby Jesus in her womb as giving Our Lady a unique experience of the Incarnation of mercy:

> She has experienced divine mercy, and has hosted the very source of this mercy in her womb: Jesus Christ. She, who has always lived intimately united with her Son, knows better than anyone what he wants: that all

men be saved, and that God's tenderness and consolation will not fail anyone. May Mary, Mother of Mercy, help us to understand how much God loves us.[22]

When we kneel at the Christmas crib and look into the face of baby Jesus, this holy sacramental puts us in the presence of mercy incarnate.

The drama of salvation

Pope Francis also sees Advent as the season in which we can deepen our appreciation of the drama of salvation that leads up to the climax of Christmas. He describes salvation history as consisting of a series of "phases", like acts in a play; "history is made step by step: God makes history".[23] The Incarnation - "God's coming into history" - introduces "the last hour" of salvation history (*1 Jn* 2:18) during which we anticipate "the final phase" which "will be of the second and definitive Coming of Christ".[24]

The beginning of salvation history - the fall of man

When talking about the drama of salvation during Advent, Pope Francis begins with the fall of man and original sin. The history of salvation begins with a catastrophe from whose consequences the human race still suffers. Created for friendship with our creator, God invited our first parents to intimate communion with himself and clothed them with resplendent grace and justice. Our first parents, tempted by the devil, let their trust in their creator die in their hearts and, abusing their freedom, disobeyed God's command - the original sin. (*Gn* 3:1-11; *Rm* 5:19). After the first sin, the world is virtually inundated by sin. The history of the human race since the first sin has been a history of living and dying from the consequences. The tragedy is that we know deep in our hearts that things could have been so different. The Church has come to understand this history through the doctrine of original sin. The Holy Father explains that because of original sin our nature is wounded:

> It's something we know from experience. Our humanity is wounded; wc know how to distinguish between good and evil, we know what is evil, we try to follow the path of goodness, but we often fall because of our weaknesses and choose evil. This is a consequence of original sin…something that actually happened at the origins of mankind.[25]

The beginning of salvation history is situated in the fact that God did not abandon the human race after our Fall. The Church identifies God's first revelation of his mysterious plan to save the human race in a passage of the Book of Genesis, called the *Protoevangelium* ["the first gospel"] (*Gn* 3:15), which brings us into the heart of Advent and the mystery of Christmas, "the first announcement of the Messiah and Redeemer, of a battle between the serpent and the Woman, and of the final victory of a descendant of hers". (*CCC* 410-411):

> I will put make you enemies of each other,
> you and the woman,
> your offspring and her offspring.
> It will crush your head,
> and you will strike its heel. (*Gn* 3:15)

After the fall, humanity is not abandoned by God. He did not cease his revelation to us, but his first gospel promises salvation for all from sin, from the bite of the snake, the devil. As Pope Francis puts it, "we are not cursed, nor are we abandoned to ourselves. The ancient account of God's first love for man and woman already had fire written into its pages in this regard!"[26]

The God of Abraham, Isaac and Jacob

The Old Testament is the story of God's journey with his people, as he acts to break through the alienation, incomprehension and hostility caused by our history of sin, and our propensity to commit personal sins. Reflecting on the genealogy of Jesus in St Matthew's Gospel, Pope Francis reflects:

> It was a journey that began long ago, in Paradise, immediately after the original sin. God had this idea: to make the journey with us. Therefore he called Abraham, the first person indicated on this list, and he invited him to walk. Abraham began the journey: he begot Isaac, and Isaac begot Jacob, and Jacob begot Judah. And so

it went, over the course of history. God journeys with his people because he did not want to come and save us apart from history; he wanted to make history with us.[27]

Since the days of the early Church, Christians have called Abraham our "Father in faith", "those who belong to the faith of Abraham who is the father of us all" (*Rm* 4:16). As the priest says every time he prays the First Eucharistic Prayer:

> Be pleased to look upon these offerings with a serene and kindly countenance, and to accept them, as once you were pleased to accept the gifts of your servant Abel the just, the sacrifice of Abraham, our father in faith.

Pope Francis wants us to realise that we are part of a "thread of hope" that can be traced back to its beginning with God's promise to Abraham.

Abraham was a man of faith, belief and obedience

The *Catechism of the Catholic Church* presents two biblical figures as essential to salvation history - Abraham and Mary. The faith of both mark significant phases in the progress of salvation history:

> By faith, he lived as a stranger and pilgrim in the Promised Land. By faith, Sarah was given to conceive the son of the promise. And by faith Abraham offered his only son in sacrifice. (*CCC* 145)

The Virgin Mary most perfectly embodies the obedience of faith. By faith Mary welcomes the tidings and promise brought by the angel Gabriel, believing that "with God nothing will be impossible" and so giving her assent: "Behold I am the handmaid of the Lord; let it be [done] to me according to your word." (*CCC* 148)

Time and again Pope Francis exhorts us to be people of faith like Abraham and Mary, placing all our trust in God. Abraham is "the man who left his land without knowing where he was going. He left in obedience, in faithfulness; the man who believed in the Word of God and was justified in that faith".[28]

The Annunciation to the Blessed Virgin Mary

Pope Francis describes the Annunciation to the Blessed Virgin Mary as "a definitive step along the journey of salvation since man first departed the garden of paradise".[29] It is the definitive step in salvation history because during the Annunciation the Incarnation of the Son of God occurred. And the Incarnation occurs during the "fiat" of Mary, the "yes" of Mary that shows her to be "the purest realisation of faith" (*CCC* 149):

"The Holy Spirit will come upon you" the angel answered "and the power of the Most High will cover you with its shadow. And so the child will be holy and will be called Son of God. Know this too: your kinswoman Elizabeth has, in her old age, herself conceived a son; and she whom people called barren is now in her sixth month. For nothing is impossible to God". "I am the handmaid of the Lord," said Mary. "Let what you have said be done to me." And the angel left her. (*Lk* 1:35-38)

St Luke's account of Mary's "yes" shows that Mary is able to make a true assent of faith, that is, she undertakes a real role of co-operation with the will of God. She is not an automaton who is compelled to do as God wants and who could not have refused. However, this faith has to be understood within the context of Mary being "full of grace". God's grace is essential for allowing Mary to give her assent:

> She was so filled with grace that from her soul grace poured into her flesh from which was conceived the Son of God. Hugh of St Victor says of this: "Because the love of the Holy Spirit so inflamed her soul, he worked a wonder in her flesh, in that from it was born God made Man." "And therefore also the Holy which shall be born of you shall be called the Son of God" (*Lk* 1:35). (St Thomas Aquinas, *On the Angelic Salutation*)

Mary's "yes" was the culmination
of a history of "yeses" to God

Pope Francis sees Mary's "yes" as the culmination of a
series of yeses to God throughout salvation history that
countered Adam and Eve's disobedience. He calls the
Annunciation "the feast of 'yes'". The Holy Father exhorts
us to be people of the "yes". When people do not want to
say "yes" to God, they usually do not say "no", they just
hide like Adam and Eve did after they sinned.

God then called our father Abraham: "Go forth from
your land, from your home". And Abraham obeyed,
he said "yes" to the Lord, and he left his land without
knowing where he was to go. This is the people's first
"yes" to God. It is here, with Abraham, that God - who
watched his people - began to "walk with". He walked
with Abraham: "Walk before me", God said to him…
Today the Gospel tells us that at the end of this chain
of "yeses" is the beginning of another "yes" which is
starting to grow: the "yes" of Mary. It is with this "yes"
that God not only watches how man is doing, he not only
walks with his people, but becomes one of us and takes
on our flesh. In fact Mary's "yes" opens the door to the
"yes" of Jesus: "I come to do your will," And it is this
"yes" that goes with Jesus throughout his life, up to the
Cross: "Father, remove this cup from me; nevertheless
not my will, but thine, be done". It is in Jesus Christ

that, as Paul says to the Corinthians, there is this "yes" of God: He is the "yes"…Today is the celebration of the "yes". Indeed, in Mary's "yes" there is the "yes" of all of salvation history and there begins the ultimate "yes" of man and of God: there God re-creates, as at the beginning, with a "yes", God made the earth and man, that beautiful creation: with this "yes" I come to do your will and more wonderfully he re-creates the world, he re-creates us all. It is God's "yes" that sanctifies us, that lets us go forth in Jesus Christ. This is why today is the right day to thank the Lord and to ask ourselves: am I a man or woman of "yes" or a man or woman of "no"? Or am I a man or woman who looks away, so as not to respond? May the Lord grant us the grace to take this path of men and women who knew how to say "yes".[30]

Pope Francis's prayer for the Second Week of Advent

May Lord enable us to understand this mystery of his journey with his people in history, of his testing his chosen ones who take upon themselves their suffering, the problems, even appearing as sinners - let's think of Jesus - in order to carry on with history. Amen.[31]

Reflections: My entry into the mystery of salvation

• Do I take time to appreciate my participation in the realities of salvation history, the historical reality of the mysteries of Jesus Christ?

- Do I learn from the "heavenly wisdom" revealed in Abraham to live in faith, hope and obedience?

- Do I learn from the "heavenly wisdom" revealed in Mary to seek faith to untie the knot of sin in my life and live in obedience to God?

- Am I a person of the "yes" to God?

Ask the Holy Spirit for the grace to live in the "yes" of salvation history.

THIRD WEEK OF ADVENT
The joy of meeting Jesus

Prayers for the Third Week of Advent

O God, who see how your people
faithfully await the feast of the Lord's Nativity,
enable us, we pray,
to attain the joys of so great a salvation
and to celebrate them always
with solemn worship and glad rejoicing.

Collect for Third Sunday of Advent

Unworthy servants that we are, O Lord,
grieved by the guilt of our deeds,
we pray that you may gladden us
by the saving advent of your Only Begotten Son.

Collect for Thursday, Third Week of Advent

Intention for the Third Week of Advent

There is no better time than the Third Week of Advent to
follow the Holy Father's advice about seeking the joy of
meeting Jesus. The Holy Father wants us to look forward
with expectancy to celebrate the Christmas "joys of so
great a salvation". Humbly aware of our sinfulness, and

"grieved by the guilt of our deeds", we ask for the grace of experiencing the joy of the "saving advent" of God's Only Begotten Son.

Rejoice, the Lord is near

The Third Sunday of Advent is also known as Gaudete Sunday, after the first word of the introit, (the opening antiphon) *Gaudete*, "Rejoice": "Rejoice in the Lord always; again I say, rejoice. Indeed the Lord is near". (*Ph* 4:4-5). Pope Francis explains the significance of Gaudete Sunday like this:

> In the liturgy, the invitation to rejoice, to arise, resounds repeatedly, because the Lord is near, Christmas is near. The Christian message is called the "gospel", that is, "good news", an announcement of joy for all people; the Church is not a haven for sad people, the Church is a joyful home![32]

In Rome, Gaudete Sunday is also known as Bambinelli Sunday. Thousands of children fill St Peter's Square with laughter and excitement and hold up their statues of baby Jesus (known as Bambinelli) for the Holy Father to bless from his window. Pope Benedict XVI explained the significance of Bambinelli Sunday, which highlights the joy at the heart of Gaudete Sunday:

> The blessing of the "Bambinelli" as they are called in Rome, reminds us that the crib is a school of life where

we can learn the secret of true joy. This does not consist in having many things but in feeling loved by the Lord, in giving oneself as a gift for others and in loving one another. Let us look at the crib. Our Lady and St Joseph do not seem to be a very fortunate family; their first child was born in the midst of great hardship; yet they are full of deep joy, because they love each other, they help each other and, especially, they are certain that God, who made himself present in the little Jesus, is at work in their story. And the shepherds? What did they have to rejoice about? That Newborn Infant was not to change their condition of poverty and marginalisation. But faith helped them recognise the "babe wrapped in swaddling clothes and lying in a manger" as a "sign" of the fulfilment of God's promises for all human beings, "with whom he is pleased" (*Lk* 2: 12, 14).[33]

Pope Francis sees joy, especially during times of suffering, as a sign of being open to the Holy Spirit. He wrote an apostolic exhortation called *The Joy of the Gospel* that mentions joy one hundred and ten times. His opening sentence is:

> The joy of the gospel fills the hearts and lives of all who encounter Jesus. Those who accept his offer of salvation are set free from sin, sorrow, inner emptiness and loneliness. With Christ joy is constantly born anew.[34]

Since the coming of the Holy Spirit at Pentecost, Christians have known that joy is one of the fruits of the Holy Spirit, a gift from God that we experience irrespective of the circumstances of our lives. It comes to us when we are close to God in our day to day lives. This joyful fruit of the Holy Spirit also gives peace of mind and objectivity.

For Pope Francis, and other guides to the spiritual life, this experience of joy irrespective of the circumstances of our lives is a sign of living a genuine Christian life. As he explained on Gaudete Sunday:

> Christian joy, like hope, is founded on God's fidelity, on the certainty that he always keeps his promises. The Prophet Isaiah exhorts those who have lost their way and have lost heart to entrust themselves to the faithfulness of the Lord, for his salvation will not delay in bursting into their lives. All those who have encountered Jesus along the way experience a serenity and joy in their hearts which nothing and no one can take away. Our joy is Jesus Christ, his faithful love is inexhaustible! Therefore, when a Christian becomes sad, it means that he has distanced himself from Jesus. But then we must not leave him alone! We should pray for him, and make him feel the warmth of the community.[35]

A great example of the power of Christian joy is the twentieth century martyr Blessed Karl Leisner. Blessed Karl Leisner suffered from tuberculosis and was imprisoned in Dachau concentration camp. However, amidst the cruel deprivations and inhumanity of the Nazi concentration camp, Karl Leisner was known for his joy. Fr Otto Pies SJ wrote an account of Blessed Karl Leisner celebrating Christmas Vigil Mass with fellow inmate priests:

> Radiant and blissful, he chanted the Gospel of the good news of great joy "which shall be to all the people". It was an unforgettable experience for many of us to observe with what a deep, moving devotion and joy the deacon discharged the duties of his holy office on this eve of Christmas. There reigned a childlike rejoicing among the participants in spite of the surrounding reality. Seldom had one seen men as joyful and happy as these prisoners who in blissful joy embraced each other and wished each other good luck in the darkness of the camp streets or in the poverty of their rooms. The most joyous among the joy-filled men was Karl Leisner; for he had been so near to the Divine Child in the form of bread and wine and had been permitted to celebrate the mystery of love with him.[36]

Christianity is the history of a growing joy

Pope Francis sees this joy beginning with Abraham, a joy that has grown among Christians through history. Abraham's joy comes from "believing against all hope, that he should become the father of many nations". He hoped and believed in God's promise, despite all the signs to the contrary:

> Thus when there is no human hope, there is this virtue which leads you forward. It is humble and simple, but it gives you joy, sometimes great joy, sometimes simply peace. However, we can always be certain that hope does not disappoint. Abraham's joy grows in history. "Your father Abraham rejoiced that he was to see my day". (*Jn* 8:56). It's true that hope is sometimes hidden, it is unseen and sometimes it is openly manifest. Thus, upon Mary's arrival at her cousin's house, Elizabeth says to her: "as soon as I heard your voice, the babe in my womb leaped for joy!" (*Lk* 1:44). In this meeting there is the joy of the presence of God who walks with his people and when there is joy, there is peace. This is the virtue of hope: from joy to peace, which never disappoints.[37]

Abraham's joy reaches a crescendo in the rejoicing of the Annunciation, the alleluia of the angel hosts at Bethlehem, the Beatitudes of Our Lord, and the joy of the Resurrection, Ascension and Pentecost. We live in this crescendo of joy made possible by the "yes" of Abraham and Mary.

Pope Francis sees Mary first and foremost as a woman of joy, with a life that proclaims the joy to be found in being close to God. "Rejoice!" is the angel's greeting to Mary (*Lk* 1:28) and Mary's visit to Elizabeth makes John leap for joy in his mother's womb (Lk 1:41). In her song of praise, Mary proclaims: "My spirit rejoices in God my Saviour". (*Lk* 1:47).

Mary is also the cause of our joy because she is the mother of Jesus, who comes into our lives to free us from the slavery and misery of sin. Pope Francis says:

> The life of one who has discovered Jesus is filled with an inner joy so great that nothing and no one can take it away. Christ gives to his own the strength necessary to be neither sad nor disheartened, when problems seem unsolvable.[38]

The Holy Father wants us to realise that we can experience joy, even when life is hard, even unbearable, if we remain close to Jesus through Our Lady. During the Third Week of Advent Pope Francis encourages us to pray to Our Lady asking her help so that we meet Jesus this Christmas:

> May the Virgin Mary help us to hasten our steps to Bethlehem, to encounter the Child who is born for us, for the salvation and joy of all people. To her the angel said: "Hail, full of grace: the Lord is with you" (*Lk* 1:28). May she obtain for us the grace to live the joy of the gospel in our families, at work, in the parish and everywhere. An intimate joy, fashioned of wonder and tenderness. The joy a mother experiences when she looks at her newborn baby and feels that he or she is a gift from God, a miracle for which she can only give thanks![39]

The joy of encountering Jesus

Pope Francis wants us to understand that the purpose of our lives is personally to encounter Jesus. He sees Advent as the opportunity not to miss out on the whole purpose of our lives, because Advent is the season during which "we journey to meet him, to encounter him with our hearts and our lives, to meet him, the living One, as he is; to meet him in faith".[40]

Every day in Advent is an opportunity to prepare for this encounter with the person of Jesus. But Pope Francis knows that for this encounter with Jesus to happen we must journey with the expectation that we'll really and truly meet him. The Holy Father wants us to take advantage of the graces open to us during Advent to strengthen our hope of meeting Jesus now. We must abandon thinking that this encounter is postponed until after death, and truly have faith that we'll meet Jesus in the sacraments and prayer:

> We could ask ourselves this question: But when do I meet Jesus? Only at the end? No, no! We meet him every day. How? In prayer, when you pray, you meet Jesus. When you receive Communion, you meet Jesus in the Sacraments. When you bring your child to be baptised, you meet Jesus, you find Jesus. And today, you who are receiving Confirmation, you too will encounter Jesus; then you will meet him in Communion.[41]

Steps to take during Advent to encounter Jesus

Pope Francis recommends that we take a number of steps that will help us encounter Jesus:

Trust Jesus and let him encounter you

Pope Francis is convinced that we can block a genuine encounter with Jesus because we don't trust Our Lord enough and we want to remain in control. It's a fundamental mistake only to want to meet Jesus on our own terms, because it betrays a failure really to acknowledge that he is God. When we seek Jesus only on our own terms Pope Francis describes us as wanting to be "masters of the moment". We want to be in control of meeting Jesus, we want to be masters of the moment. But the truth is that we can only encounter Jesus by having faith enough to allow him to be the master of the moment. Commenting on the faith of the centurion in Matthew 8:5-11, Pope Francis says,

> The centurion made a journey to meet the Lord, but he made it in faith. He not only encountered the Lord, but he came to know the joy of being encountered by him. And this is precisely the sort of encounter we desire, the encounter of faith. To encounter the Lord, but also to allow ourselves to be encountered by him. This is very important. When we go out to meet the Lord we in some sense are masters of the moment. However, when

we allow ourselves to be encountered by him, he enters into us and renews us from within. This is what it means for Christ to come: to renew all things, to renew hearts, souls, lives, hope and the journey.[42]

Don't pretend you're not a sinner

Another block to encountering Jesus is not being honest about one's own sinfulness, our own personal history of sinful actions, habits and attitudes. If we don't admit that we're sinners, how can Our Lord Jesus Christ save us? Pope Francis wants each one of us to have a personal history of salvation, and like Israel we need to have the humility to admit we're sinners who need saving. Once the people of Israel admitted they were sinners who needed to be saved, God was able to enter history and transform man's history of sin into God's history of salvation. We need to allow God to "write our history":[43]

To encounter Jesus also means allowing oneself to be gazed upon by him. "But, Father, you know," one of you might say to me, "you know that this journey is horrible for me, I am such a sinner, I have committed many sins...how can I encounter Jesus?" And you know that the people whom Jesus most sought out were the greatest sinners; and they reproached him for this, and the people - those who believed themselves righteous - would say: this is no true prophet, look what lovely company he keeps! He was with sinners...And he said: I came for those in need of salvation, in need of healing. Jesus heals our sins. And along the way Jesus comes and forgives us - all of us sinners, we are all sinners - even when we make a mistake, when we commit a sin, when we sin. And this forgiveness that we receive in Confession is an encounter with Jesus. We always encounter Jesus.[44]

Expect Jesus to disturb you

Pope Francis is certain that if your life is safe and comfortable, then you haven't met Our Lord Jesus Christ. Christians who want to be encountered by Jesus cannot make their life goals comfort and safety: "How much damage does the comfortable life, well-being, do? The gentrification of the heart paralyses us."[45] Being a Christian means going out of our comfort zone, and allowing God to disturb us:

The Lord bothers us in order to make history, He makes us go so many times on the path that we don't want... That is why for God, making history with his people means walking and putting his chosen ones to the test. Indeed, in general, his chosen ones went through dark, painful, bad times, like these that we have seen; but in the end the Lord comes...Let us always remember to say, with trust, even in the worst of times, even in moments of illness, when we realise that we have to ask for extreme unction because there is no way out: "Lord, history did not begin with me nor will it end with me. You go on, I'm ready".[46]

We need silence to encounter the mystery of God

During Advent we need to find times of silence in order to encounter the mystery of God and the mystery of ourselves. God awaits us in the depths of our hearts. (*Gaudium et Spes* 14) Pope Francis wants us to realise that God guards the intimate and personal mystery of both himself and ourselves. He sees an example of this expressed in the angel Gabriel's Annunciation to the Blessed Virgin Mary, "The power of the Most High will overshadow you. The Holy Spirit will come upon you". (*Lk* 1:26-38) It is in this cloud of mystery that we will encounter Jesus:

> Throughout salvation history, the overshadowing of God has always guarded mystery. The overshadowing of God accompanied his people in the desert and the whole of salvation history demonstrates that the Lord has always guarded the mystery. He veiled the mystery, he did not publicise the mystery. In fact a mystery that promotes itself is not Christian, it is not a mystery of God. The day's Gospel clearly confirms this for when Mary received the angel's announcement, the mystery of her motherhood remained hidden. God's

overshadowing of us in our lives helps us to discover our own mystery: our mystery of encounter with the Lord, the mystery of our life's journey with the Lord. In fact, each of us knows how mysteriously the Lord works in his or her heart and soul. And this is the overshadowing, the power, the Holy Spirit's style, as it were, for veiling our mystery. This overshadowing in us, in our lives, is called silence. Silence is the cloud that veils the mystery of our relationship with the Lord, of our holiness and of our sins.[47]

Pope Francis's prayer for the Third Week of Advent

Lord, grant us all the grace to love silence this Advent, to seek it out, to have a heart guarded by the cloud of silence. Thus the mystery growing within us shall bear much fruit. Amen.[48]

Reflections: My joy in meeting Jesus

- Do I live a life filled with joy?

- Do I believe I will, and do I, encounter Jesus with joy?

- In prayer?

- In communion?

- In the other sacraments, (reconciliation, confirmation, anointing, bringing children (others) to be baptised)?

- Do I trust Jesus and let him encounter me (to renew me from within)?

- Am I honest about my own sinfulness so I can have the joy of letting Christ save me?

- Do I let Jesus disturb me from a "safe and comfortable" life?

- Do I find times of silence in order to encounter the mystery of God and rejoice in his presence?

Ask the Holy Spirit for the grace to live the joy of the gospel in our families, at work, in the parish and everywhere.

Fourth Week of Advent
The Wonder of the Incarnation

Prayers for the Fourth Week of Advent

Drop down dew from above, you heavens,
and let the clouds rain down the Just One;
let the earth be opened and bring forth a Saviour.

Entrance Antiphon for the Fourth Sunday of Advent

O God, who through the child-bearing of the holy Virgin
graciously revealed the radiance of your glory
   to the world,
grant, we pray,
that we may venerate with integrity of faith
the mystery of so wondrous an Incarnation
and always celebrate it with due reverence.

Collect for 19th December, Fourth Week of Advent

Intention for the Fourth Week of Advent

During the Fourth Week of Advent, Pope Francis guides us
to a deeper understanding of the mystery of the Incarnation
of the Son of God. May we grow in appreciation of the
gentle humility of the littleness of the Incarnation, like

"dew from above", that "lets the clouds rain down the Just One". By so doing, we prepare to "venerate with integrity of faith the mystery of so wondrous an Incarnation".

The O Antiphons

During the Fourth Week of Advent, the Church proclaims the "O Antiphons" during Vespers to celebrate the wonder of the Incarnation. Since the Second Vatican Council, the O Antiphons have also been adapted as the "Alleluia" verse of the Masses for the Fourth Week of Advent.

What are the O Antiphons? Otherwise known as "the Great Os", they are seven verses drawn from the Old Testament associated with the advent of the promised Messiah. They are called the O Antiphons because each of the seven begins will the interjection "O": O Wisdom, O Lord, O Root of Jesse, O Key of David, O Daystar, O King of the Nations, O God-with-us (in Latin, O Sapientia, O Adonai, O Radix Jesse, O Clavis, O Oriens, O Rex Gentium, O Emmanuel). Fr John Zuhlsdorf refers to them as "fervent prayers asking Our Lord to come to us".[49] The first letters of the Latin words when spelt out backwards from 24th December (Christmas Eve) are: **E**mmanuel, **R**ex, **O**riens, **C**lavis, **R**adix, **A**donai, **S**apientia. They spell out the Latin phrase *ero cras*, "I come tomorrow", referring to Christ's birth on Christmas Day.

Come, Lord!

Pope Francis invites us to pray the O Antiphons with the expectancy and hope of Israel waiting for the coming of the Messiah and the Church earnestly praying since the early days of Christianity for the Second Coming of the Lord. The final words that Our Lord speaks in revelation are "I shall indeed be with you soon" and the Church replies, "Amen; come, Lord Jesus!" [Maranatha] (*Rv* 22:20).

At every celebration of the Holy Sacrifice of the Mass we pray in the Eucharistic Acclamations with this expectation and hope for the Lord's coming:

> We proclaim your Death, O Lord,
> and profess your Resurrection
> until you come again.

> When we eat this Bread and drink this Cup,
> we proclaim your Death, O Lord,
> until you come again.

During Advent our heartfelt prayer for the coming of the Lord should grow in intensity through our awareness of the wonder of the Incarnation. Pope Francis describes the O Antiphons as the Church calling out to the Lord, "Come, Lord" because she is awaiting the birth of our Saviour:

> In this final week before Christmas the Church repeats the prayer, 'Come, Lord!' and she calls out to the Lord with various and different names: O Wisdom, O Root of

Jesse, O Dayspring, O King of the Nations, and today, O Emmanuel. This week the Church is like Mary: she is awaiting a birth. The Virgin sensed within herself, in body and in soul that the birth of her child was near. [And he added:] surely in her heart she said to the baby she was carrying in her womb: "Come, I want to see your face, for they have told me you will be great!" This Church lives this spiritually, for we accompany Our Lady in this journey of waiting and we too wish to hasten the Lord's birth. This is the reason for the Church's prayer: "Come, O Key of David, O Dayspring, O Wisdom, O Emmanuel". This invocation recalls the final words in the Sacred Scripture; in the last lines of the Book of Revelation, the Church cries out: "Come, Lord Jesus", Maranatha, which may indicate a desire or a certainty: the Lord is coming.[50]

Is our soul open for the coming of the Lord?

The Holy Father encourages us during the last week of Advent to prepare ourselves for the Lord's coming to our hearts and souls this Christmas. He invites us to share in Our Lady's expectation for the coming of the Lord by praying the O Antiphons with real feeling. He sees the O Antiphons as an examination of conscience, a moment to discern if our hearts are truly open for the coming of the Lord:

It is a prayer that allows us to examine if our soul communicates to others that it does not wish to be disturbed, or if instead it is an open soul, a great soul ready to receive the Lord. A soul that already feels what the Church will tell us tomorrow in the Antiphon: Know that today the Lord comes and tomorrow you shall behold his glory.[51]

Pope Francis's examination of conscience for the Fourth Week of Advent

What is happening within us?

Are we watching or are we closed? Are we vigilant or are we safe and secure in an inn, no longer wanting to continue on? Are we pilgrims or are we wandering?

Is there room for the Lord, or is there only room for celebration, for shopping, for making noise?

Are our souls open, as the soul of Holy Mother Church is open, and as Mary's soul was open? Or have we closed our souls and put a highly erudite note on the door saying: please do not disturb?[52]

Pope Francis encourages us make the O Antiphons our heartfelt prayer because he knows that the coming of Our Lord into our hearts and souls is not some pious metaphor, but is the most profound and life-changing reality. Christ wants to dwell in our hearts (*Jn* 14:23). Many of the saints knew the truth of Jesus coming to dwell in our hearts, using the image of Christ being born within us to convey this reality. Blessed Titus Brandsma, the Carmelite martyr wrote, "unite ourselves to Mary, so that God should be conceived in us also, and brought forth by us. It is our task to bear God as she bore him". Another Carmelite martyr, St Teresa Benedicta of the Cross (Edith Stein), wrote, "Now my heart has become a crib waiting for Mary's Son. She gives me her newly born Child to lay in my heart". And Blessed Columba Marmion, the Benedictine, wrote, "we will have the immense joy of seeing Christ born anew within our hearts".

During this final week of Advent, pray for the grace that your soul comes to resemble Mary and the Church:

> In fact, the Lord comes twice. His first coming is what we are about to commemorate, his physical birth. Then, he will come at the end of time, at the close of history. However, St Bernard tells us that there is a third coming of the Lord: his coming to us each day: each day, the Lord visits his Church. He visits each one of us. And our soul also enters into this likeness: our soul comes to resemble the Church; our soul comes to resemble Mary. Therefore, our souls are waiting in anticipation for the coming of the Lord, open souls calling out: Come, Lord! Over the course of these days the Holy Spirit moves in the heart of each one of us, forming this prayer within us: come, come![53]

Only the humble understand

Pope Francis also advises us to pray the O Antiphons with genuine humility because he knows that only the humble can know and love the humility of our incarnate God.

> How important are the beautiful O Antiphons that the Church has us pray over the course of these days: O Son of David, O Adonai, O Wisdom, O Root of Jesse, O Emmanuel, come and give us life, come and save us, for only you can, alone I cannot. It is with this humility, the humility of the desert, the humility of the barren soul, that we receive grace: the grace to blossom, to bear fruit and to give life.[54]

Only when we realise the barrenness of our sinfulness and our powerlessness to save ourselves can Jesus be born in our hearts. Only honest humility about our spiritual poverty can give God the freedom of action he needs to bring life and fruitfulness to our souls. By stressing this, Pope Francis is advocating the spirituality of the Old Testament, of the Poor Ones of the Lord:

> The People of the "poor" - those who, humble and meek, rely solely on their God's mysterious plans, who await the justice, not of men but of the Messiah - are in the end the great achievement of the Holy Spirit's hidden mission during the time of the promises that prepare for Christ's coming. It is this quality of heart, purified and enlightened by the Spirit, which is expressed in

the Psalms. In these poor, the Spirit is making ready "a people prepared for the Lord." (*CCC* 716)

Fr Albert Gelin in his seminal work on the *'anawim*, *The Poor of YHWH*, makes the reasonable proposition that Jesus grew up in an *'anawim* family, immersed in the *'anawim* culture. During his early life he is surrounded by the *anaw*, the devout poor, Joseph and Mary, Zechariah and Elizabeth, Simeon and Anna, and John the Baptist. Fr Gelin describes Mary, and her Song of Poverty (the Magnificat) as the "perfect consummation" of Israel's faith:

> Let us not forget that when the bridge had been made between the Old Testament and the New, Mary greeted the Messianic age with her Magnificat, which repeats the words and themes dear to the *'anawim*. Mary is the culmination of this mystic tradition, which is in a way the heart of the Bible. The Magnificat is more than a fabric woven of Old Testament quotations. In it we hear the woman who has so identified herself with the *'anawim* that, conscious of the newness of the Incarnation, she has become their perfect and living expression. (Albert Gelin, *Key Concepts of the Old Testament*, p. 93; *The Poor of YHWH*, p.94).

Our Lady's Magnificat identifies the human self-sufficiencies - pride, power and riches - as diametrically opposing the virtues of God's poor ones, the *'anawim* -

humility, weakness and poverty. By identifying humility, weakness and poverty as essential for human devotion to God and observance of a moral life, the 'anawim, inspired by the Holy Spirit, not only hit upon the three things necessary for authentic spirituality, they also identified qualities chosen as necessary by God:

> Jesus chose poverty, suffering, failure in his Incarnation, in his public life, in his Passion. These "pure scandals, these foolish things...God accepts and God wants; and because they prevail in the humanity he personally assumed, they have become the most divine of human realities." (Albert Gelin, *The Poor of YHWH*, pp.100-101, quoting Fr P Regamey).

The difference between the 'anawim's choice and Jesus's choice, is that the 'anawim accept humility, weakness and poverty out of a sense of human sinfulness before the holiness of God, while Jesus accepts humility, weakness and poverty out of self-giving love for us, because being truly God and truly human he was sinless.

The early Church interpreted Jesus's Incarnation and life, especially his birth in the manger and his Passion and crucifixion, as a "mystery of poverty" (Gelin). We see this in the wonderful Christological poem of Philippians:

> In your minds you must be the same as Christ Jesus: his state was divine, yet he did not cling to his equality with God, but emptied himself, to assume the condition of a

> slave, and became as men are; and being as all men are, he was humbler yet, even to accepting death, death on a cross. (*Ph* 2:5-8).

In the *'anawim* we hear the Word of God growing louder and louder the nearer he comes, until he is clearly spoken in the cry of a baby in the poverty of a stable in Bethlehem and the cry of the man on the Cross, expressing the astonishing humility of God, accepted out of love of mankind.

The humility of the Incarnation

Pope Francis wants us to realise that the Son of God becoming incarnate as a vulnerable and powerless baby was not just a necessary step for Jesus to grow into a man, but that baby Jesus reveals an essential truth about God and about what it means to be truly human:

> In the face of little Jesus we contemplate the face of God, who does not reveal himself in strength and power but in the weakness and frailty of a newborn babe. This is what our God is like, he comes so close, in a child. This Child reveals the faithfulness and tenderness of the unconditional love with which God surrounds each one of us. That is why we celebrate at Christmas, thus reliving what the shepherds at Bethlehem experienced.[55]

The Holy Father believes that in order to enter the mystery of the Incarnation - why God assumed a human nature - we have to understand who man is, who each one of us is. In our pride and ego we often make the mistake of thinking we're powerful and all important. This can so distort our view of ourselves that we assume we're the masters of our own lives and, in the most extreme cases, masters of the world. But the truth is from God's perspective we are always creatures created by him from the elements of the earth, into which he breathes each one of our souls. Pope Francis likes a passage from the Prophet Isaiah:

> For I, the Lord, your God,
> I am holding you by the right hand;
> I tell you, "Do not be afraid,
> I will help you."

> Do not be afraid, Jacob, poor worm,
> Israel, puny mite.
> I will help you - it is the Lord who speaks;
> the Holy One of Israel is your Redeemer. (*Is* 41: 13-14)

Pope Francis explains that in this passage the Lord says: "worm of Jacob, you are like a little worm to me, you are little but I love you very much".[56] God choose Israel (Jacob) not because they were a great and powerful nation, but quite the opposite, God choose Israel because "they were the smallest of all, the poorest of all. God is truly in love with this poverty, with this littleness".[57]

God becomes little so that he can come close to the little, so that he can come close to you and me. The Holy

Father describes this as being like a mum or dad bending down and making themselves small to get close to their kids to sing them a lullaby. God is like a parent who speaks baby talk:

> Jesus speaks to us in the same way. He draws near to us. When we look at a father or mother draw close to their children, we see that they make themselves small, they speak with a child's voice and communicate with a child's gestures. Whoever sees them from the outside might think they look ridiculous. However, the love of a father and mother needs to draw close, to bend down to the child's world. And even if the father or mother were to speak to their child in the normal way, the child would understand, but they want to take on the child's way of speaking; they draw near. They make themselves children, as it were. And so it is with the Lord. The Greek philosophers, in speaking about this, used a very difficult word: syncatabasis, the divine condescension whereby God accepts becoming one of us. The Lord speaks to us in this way. He acts as parents do with their children.[58]

God made himself small

The wonder of the Incarnation is that God who is Spirit, Infinite, Eternal and Divine became matter, finite, time-bound and human. God the uncreated assumed a created nature. God made himself small, accepting the littleness of the human condition. Jesus lived a fully human existence, with its range of emotions and limitations. As Fr Gerald O'Collins puts it, through the Incarnation the Son of God experiences at first hand what it is to be human - with all our physical and psychological strengths and weaknesses.

This has consequences for God and consequences for us. For God, it means God has lived a human life from the "inside", and knows, through direct participation, what it means to be a creature in his creation. The other consequences must remain mysteries to us, because how can we know what it means to be God living a human life? The consequences for us are many and profound. First, that God choose to assume a human nature must mean we're really special and important to him, and that he loves us beyond anything we can imagine. It also means that because he has expressed himself through a human life, we have privileged access to his presence and his thoughts, because it is far easier for us to understand another human being than to understand God, an eternal Spirit.

As Fr O'Collins puts it, Jesus is able to show us what leading a human life in the presence of God should really be like. We don't have to make wild guesses or make it up as we go along! Simply put, the Incarnation means that the Creator of the universe loves each one of us, and is on our side. We are all worthwhile and lovable, because as St John realised:

> God loved the world so much that he gave his only Son, so that everyone who believes in him may not be lost but may have eternal life. (*Jn* 3:16).

Pope Francis explains the significance of God becoming small this way:

> Jesus comes not as an army general, not as a powerful ruler. He will instead sprout, as a shoot, like in the First Reading from the Prophet Isaiah (11:1-10): "There shall come forth a shoot from the stump of Jesse". He is a shoot, he is humble, he is meek, and he has come for the humble, for the meek, to bring salvation to the sick, to the poor, to the oppressed, as he himself says in the Fourth Chapter of Luke, when he is in the Synagogue in Nazareth. And Jesus has come for the marginalised: he marginalised himself; he does not have a non-negotiable value, being equal to God. Indeed, he humbled himself, he debased himself. He became an outcast, he humiliated himself in order to give us the mystery of the Father and his own.[59]

We can only get close to Jesus by becoming little

If we want to get closer to Jesus and enter more deeply into the wonder of the Incarnation we must follow the way of littleness. The New Testament is clear that it is only those who have the humility to accept the vulnerability, poverty and powerlessness of being human that can encounter Jesus:

> At that time Jesus exclaimed, "I bless you, Father, Lord of heaven and of earth, for hiding these things from the learned and the clever and revealing them to mere children". (*Mt* 11:25)

> It was to shame the wise that God chose what is foolish by human reckoning, and to shame the strong that he chose what is weak by human reckoning; those whom the world thinks common and contemptible are the ones God has chosen - those who are nothing at all to show up those who are everything. The human race has nothing to boast about to God. (*1 Co* 1: 27-29)

Pope Francis encourages us to live a spirituality of littleness so that we can meet Jesus, because only by accepting who we truly are will we avoid blocking God who makes himself small to get close to us:

> Only those with the heart of babes are capable of receiving this revelation. Only those with a humble, meek heart, which feels the need to pray, to open up to God, to feel poor have this capacity. In a word, only those who go forth with the first beatitude: the poor in spirit. For only this poverty is capable of receiving the revelation that the Father gives through Jesus.[60]

To walk the way of littleness, we have to have the four interrelated dispositions that we find among the poor of the Lord, the *'anawim*: "a contrite heart, one that is capable of recognising its own sins", "humility, poverty and trust in the Lord":

> When we see the holy People of God, who are humble, who have their treasure in the faith in the Lord, in the trust in the Lord; the humble, poor people who confide in the Lord, here we meet the saved ones, for this is the path that the Church must take.[61]

In the light of this, it should come as no surprise that Pope Francis's favourite saint is St Thérèse of Lisieux, the saint of the way of littleness. St Thérèse exemplifies the truth of the spiritual life that it is only when we are little that we can accept the tenderness of God:

> Do not be afraid to depend solely on the tenderness of God as St Thérèse of Lisieux did, who, for this reason, is a beloved daughter of the Blessed Mother and a great missionary saint.[62]

This Christmas the Holy Father wants us to depend solely on the tenderness of God incarnate in baby Jesus held in the arms of Mary, under the watchful eyes of St Joseph.

A prayer for the Fourth Week of Advent

Lord, lead us ever closer to your mystery, and to do so on the path that you want us to take: the path of humility, the path of meekness, the path of poverty, the path of feeling ourselves sinners. For this is how you come to save us, to free us. Amen.

Reflections: My wonder at the Incarnation

Am I waiting in expectant hope for God's second coming? Is my soul truly open for his coming now to dwell in my heart?

- What is happening within me?
- Am I watching for, or closed to, God?
- Am I vigilant, or safe and secure in an inn, no longer wanting to continue on to meet Jesus?
- Am I a pilgrim on the way, or just wandering?
- Is there room for the Lord, or is there only room for celebration, for shopping, for making noise?
- Do I accept my need for God, realising how humble, weak and poor I am before him?
- Do I follow God's way of littleness?

Pray to the Holy Spirit for the grace to blossom, to bear fruit and to give life.

CHRISTMAS

Welcoming light into our darkness

Prayers for Christmas

Today a light will shine upon us,
    for the Lord is born for us;
and he will be called Wondrous God,
Prince of peace, Father of future ages:
and his reign will be without end

Entrance Antiphon for Christmas Dawn Mass

Grant, we pray, almighty God,
that, as we are bathed in the new radiance
    of your incarnate Word,
the light of faith, which illumines our minds,
may also shine through in our deeds.

Collect for Christmas Dawn Mass

Intention for Christmas

Throughout Christmas and Christmastide, Pope Francis encourages us to welcome the light of Christ into the darkness of our sin and suffering. Light shines in the darkness because "the Lord is born for us", and we are "bathed in the new radiance", so that the "light of faith" may grow ever brighter in our lives.

Journey from darkness into light

For the past three years Pope Francis has taken a passage from the Prophet Isaiah as the primary focus for his Christmas homily:

> The people that walked in darkness
> has seen a great light;
> on those who live in a land of deep shadow,
> a light has shone. (*Is* 9:2).

The coming of the light of Christ into the darkness of the world is the culmination and fulfilment of one of the great realities and experiences of salvation history. The uncreated, holy God "whose home is in inaccessible light, whom no man has seen and no man is able to see" (*1 Tm* 6:16), whilst man, due to the fall and personal sin, lives in darkness, under thrall to the devil. Darkness is the domain of Satan, in which we sinners prefer to hide our sinful acts and sinful thoughts, "the futile works of darkness" (*Ep* 5:11).

Each one of us exists between darkness and light, damaged by the darkness introduced into human nature by original sin, and called out of darkness into God's wonderful light (cf. *1 P* 2:9). The choice is ours: to become either a child of darkness or a child of light. Pope Francis expresses the choice facing us:

> In our personal history too, there are both bright and
> dark moments, lights and shadows. If we love God and

our brothers and sisters, we walk in the light; but if our heart is closed, if we are dominated by pride, deceit, self-seeking, then darkness falls within us and around us. "Whoever hates his brother - writes the Apostle John - is in the darkness; he walks in the darkness, and does not know the way to go, because the darkness has blinded his eyes". (*1 Jn* 2:11)[63]

The profound mystery of Christmas is that God's light comes down into man's sin. To begin to appreciate the wonder of this, we have to grasp that God, in his goodness and holiness, has nothing in common with man in his wickedness and sinfulness. As St John puts it, "God is light; there is no darkness in him at all" (*1 Jn* 1:5). God is light and the darkness of man is totally alien and repugnant. But out of love for man God allows his light to shine in man's darkness. The baby Jesus is the light of God in the darkness of sin and poverty:

It is the same God that said, "Let there be light shining out of darkness", who has shone in our minds to radiate the light of the knowledge of God's glory, the glory on the face of Christ. (*2 Co* 4:6).

The mystery of God's love is revealed as even greater when one realises that not only is there a gulf between God's light and man's darkness that God chooses to bridge in order to give us his light, but that men of darkness seeing the light of God choose to reject it, and even vainly attempt to put it out:

> All that came to be had life in him, and that life was the light of men, a light that shines in the dark, a light that darkness could not overpower…On these grounds is sentence pronounced: that though the light has come into the world, men have shown they prefer darkness to the light, because their deeds were evil. And indeed, everybody who does wrong hates the light and avoids it, for fear his actions should be exposed. (*Jn* 1:4; 3:19-20).

Pope Francis's profound experience of light

Why is the image of Christ as light so important to Pope Francis? The Holy Father spoke during an interview about a profound experience of light that occurred to him during the vote that elected him pope, which he describes as a brief mystical moment in his life:

> For example, when the conclave elected me pope. Before I accepted I asked if I could spend a few minutes in the room next to the one with the balcony overlooking the square. My head was completely empty and I was seized by a great anxiety. To make it go away and relax I closed my eyes and made every thought disappear, even the thought of refusing to accept the position, as the liturgical procedure allows. I closed my eyes and

I no longer had any anxiety or emotion. At a certain point I was filled with a great light. It lasted a moment, but to me it seemed very long. Then the light faded, I got up suddenly and walked into the room where the cardinals were waiting and the table on which was the act of acceptance. I signed it, the Cardinal Camerlengo countersigned it and then on the balcony there was the "Habemus Papam" ["We have a pope"].[64]

The Holy Father has also described this experience of light as a close encounter with God that transformed his life, changing him from the shy and dour cardinal of Buenos Aires into an outgoing and exuberant Pope Francis:

On the night of my election, I had an experience of the closeness of God that gave me a great sense of interior freedom and peace, and that sense has never left me.[65]

The Light of Faith

Pope Francis's first encyclical shows the importance of the experience of the light of God to him. He gave it the title, *Lumen Fidei, The Light of Faith*. It contains one hundred and forty-two references to light:

The light of Faith: this is how the Church's tradition speaks of the great gift brought by Jesus. In John's Gospel, Christ says of himself: "I have come as light into the world, that whoever believes in me may not remain in darkness" (*Jn* 12:46). St Paul uses the same image: "God who said 'Let light shine out of darkness,' has shone in our hearts" (*2 Co* 4:6). Conscious of the immense horizon which their faith opened before them, Christians invoked Jesus as the true sun "whose rays bestow life". To Martha, weeping for the death of her brother Lazarus, Jesus said: "Did I not tell you that if you believed, you would see the glory of God?" (*Jn* 11:40). Those who believe, see; they see with a light that illumines their entire journey, for it comes from the risen Christ, the morning star which never sets.[66]

The light of faith is an ancient Christian image of the liberation of man from the darkness of sin by Our Lord through the Sacrament of Baptism. The association of Baptism and light was so strong in the early days of the Church that it was called "enlightenment":

> "This bath is called *enlightenment*, because those who receive this [catechetical] instruction are enlightened in their understanding…" Having received in Baptism the Word, "the true light that enlightens every man", the person baptised has been "enlightened", he becomes a "son of light", indeed, he becomes "light" himself. (*CCC* 1216)

This association of Baptism with enlightenment by Christ remains an important element of the rite of Baptism. After the child or adult is baptised they are presented with a candle lit from the Paschal Candle; this represents the light of Christ that has come into the life of the newly baptised. The celebrant of Baptism says:

> Receive the light of Christ. Parents and Godparents, this light is entrusted to you to be kept burning brightly. This child of yours has been enlightened by Christ. He/she is to walk always as a child of the light. May he/she keep the flame of faith alive in his/her heart. When the Lord comes, may he/she go out to meet him with all the saints in the heavenly kingdom.

Jesus is the light of the world

Since becoming pope, Francis has used the occasion of the presentation of the Christmas tree for St Peter's Square to reflect on the significance of Jesus as the light of the world. The Holy Father emphasises how the lights on the tree represent the light of Christ coming into man's world of sin and error:

> The shepherds, the Gospel says, were enfolded in a great light. Also today Jesus continues to dispel the darkness of error and sin, in order to bring mankind the joy of the divine resplendent light of which the Christmas tree is a symbol and reminder. Let us allow ourselves to be enfolded by the light of its truth, so that "the joy of the gospel fills the hearts and lives of all who encounter Jesus" (Apostolic Exhortation *Evangelii Gaudium* 1).[67]

He, the Messiah, was made man and came among us to dissipate the darkness of error and sin, bringing to humanity his divine light. Jesus will say of himself: "I am the light of the world; he who follows me will not walk in darkness, but will have the light of life" (*Jn* 8:12). Let us follow him, the true light, so as not to wander and in order, in our turn, to reflect light and warmth on those undergoing moments of difficulty and interior darkness.[68]

Welcoming the light of Christ

What is the light of Christ that we welcome into our lives at Christmas? Clearly this light is more than poetic imagery or romantic metaphor because it effects real changes in our lives, liberating us from sin, and enlightening our minds and hearts with faith. Pope Francis wants us to understand that celebration of the nativity of Our Lord is the opportunity for a special encounter with God that brings his grace into our lives:

On this night, like a burst of brilliant light, there rings out the proclamation of the Apostle: "God's grace has been revealed, and it has made salvation possible for the whole human race". (*Ti* 2:11) The grace which was revealed in our world is Jesus, born of the Virgin Mary, true man and true God. He has entered our history; he has shared our journey. He came to free us from darkness and to grant us light. In him was revealed the grace, the mercy, and the tender love of the Father: Jesus is Love incarnate.[69]

The light of Christ shining in the darkness of man's sin is God's offer to each one of us during Christmas of a deeper participation in his gift of faith. Faith is a supernatural grace from God. "Supernatural" comes from the Latin *supernaturalis*, meaning "above nature", and conveys the idea that God is above our categories, experiences and our nature. It also refers to God's free and loving gifts that raise us above what is due to our human nature and prepares us for eternal life:

> This vocation to eternal life is supernatural. It depends entirely on God's gratuitous initiative, for he alone can reveal and give himself. It surpasses the power of human intellect and will, as that of every other creature…"But, as it is written, 'What no eye has seen, nor ear heard, nor the heart of man conceived, what God has prepared for those who love him'" (*1 Co* 2:9). (*CCC* 1998)

As Fr Edward Yarnold has said, "supernatural" refers to those "gifts" by which God in sheer love raises us to a relationship with himself which is above our unaided capacity. Simply put, the "supernatural" refers to all God's initiatives that call us and enable us to lead a new life and relationship with him and each other that is above our nature as creatures; and this solely through the totally free choice and will of God. This is why it is "supernatural", that is, "above" or "beyond" the natural order of creation.

This is how St Cyril of Alexandria describes these divine gifts or graces that we receive through Our Lord's Incarnation which take us above or beyond our human nature:

> By a free concession the Son made generally available what belonged to himself alone properly and by nature…So we are raised through Christ to a dignity above our nature…For a creature, created and servant though it is, is called to what is above its nature by the sheer good pleasure and will of the Father.

The divine graces that we are offered through the Incarnation of Christ transform us into a new-born being, a new creature, a new creation, our inner nature renewed every day through our participation in the sacraments, most especially the Eucharist, and through prayer. The light of Christ transforms us so we can "be like children of light' (*Ep* 5:8).

As our baptismal candle is lit by the Paschal Candle of Christ - one flame becoming two flames - so too we are alight with the light of Christ when we remain in a state of grace. Grace conforms us into the image of Christ.

(*Rm* 8:29), re-making us in Christ (*2 Co* 5:17). In particular, this is the purpose of sacramental grace:

> Grace is first and foremost the gift of the Spirit who justifies and sanctifies us. But grace also includes the gifts that the Spirit grants us to associate us with his work, to enable us to collaborate in the salvation of others and in the growth of the Body of Christ, the Church. There are sacramental graces, gifts proper to the different sacraments. (*CCC* 2003)

We must carry the light of Christ to others

We are given the light of Christ not just to save us from sin, but so that we bring this saving light to others. A true son of the light makes the light of Christ that is present within him shine before others (*Mt* 5:14-16). Pope Francis reminds us that we are only truly Christian when we carry the light of Christ to others:

> We must carry the light of Christ with the witness of a genuine love…The Christian must be a luminous person; one who brings light, who always gives off light. A light that is not his, but a gift of God, a gift of Jesus. We carry this light! If a Christian extinguishes this light, his life has no meaning. He is a Christian in name only…I would like to ask you now, how do you want to live? As a lamp that is burning, or one that is not? Shining lamps! This is the Christian vocation![70]

The Light of the Epiphany

Pope Francis sees the feast of the Epiphany as revealing the vocation of the Church to show forth the light of Christ to the whole world. The word "epiphany" means "manifestation", showing forth. The feast of the Epiphany is the "manifestation of Jesus as Messiah of Israel, Son of God and Saviour of the world" (*CCC* 528). The Church must be a place of encounter where the peoples of the world see the light of Christ:

> We are challenged to go to Bethlehem, to find the Child and his Mother. Let us follow the light which God offers us!...The light which streams from the face of Christ, full of mercy and fidelity. And once we have found him, let us worship him with all our heart, and present him with our gifts: our freedom, our understanding and our love. True wisdom lies concealed in the face of this Child. It is here, in the simplicity of Bethlehem, that the life of the Church is summed up. For here is the wellspring of that light which draws to itself every individual and guides the journey of the peoples along the path of peace.[71]

Pope Francis's Prayer for Christmastide

May the Virgin Mary, who welcomed the Wise Men in Bethlehem, help us to lift our gaze from ourselves, to allow ourselves to be guided by the star of the gospel in order to encounter Jesus, and to be able to humble ourselves to adore him. In this way we will be able to bring to others a ray of his light, and to share with them the joy of the journey. Amen.[72]

Reflection: My welcome of light into darkness

- Am I a child of the light? A son or daughter of light?
- Do I live in the light of faith?
- Do I bring Christ's saving light to others?
- Do I worship God with all my heart and present to him the gifts of my freedom, my understanding and my love?

Pray to the Holy Spirit for his grace to collaborate in the salvation of others and in the growth of the Body of Christ.

Endnotes

[1] Morning Meditation in the Chapel of the Domus Sanctae Marthae. 2nd December 2013.

[2] "Missa Pro Ecclesia" with the Cardinal Electors, Homily of Pope Francis. 14th March 2013.

[3] Morning Meditation in the Chapel of the Domus Sanctae Marthae. 11th June 2015.

[4] Ibid.

[5] Papal Mass for the repose of the souls of the cardinals and bishops who died during the course of the year *http://www.catholicnews.com/services/englishnews/2015/those-who-give-their-lives-in-service-are-not-losers-pope-says.cfm*.

[6] Morning Meditation in the Chapel of the Domus Sanctae Marthae. 3rd May 2016.

[7] Ibid.

[8] Ibid.

[9] Ibid.

[10] Homily during pastoral visit to the parish of St Cyril of Alexandria, First Sunday of Advent. 1st December 2013.

[11] Ibid.

[12] Based on Pope Francis's Morning Meditation in the Chapel of the Domus Sanctae Marthae. 2nd December 2013.

[13] Address to the Members of the Pontifical Biblical Commission. 12th April 2013.

[14] Morning Meditation in the Chapel of the Domus Sanctae Marthae. 18th December 2014.

[15] Ibid.

[16] Morning Meditation in the Chapel of the Domus Sanctae Marthae. 17th December 2013.

[17] "Mary's Role in the Incarnation", *Communio* 30 (Spring 2003) pp.5-25.

[18] Homily for the Inauguration of the Jubilee of Mercy, 8th December 2015.

[19] Morning Meditation in the Chapel of the Domus Sanctae Marthae. 17th December 2013.

[20] Wednesday audience catechesis. 6th April 2016.

[21] Pope Benedict XVI, Regina Caeli address. 30th March 2008.

[22] Eucharistic celebration on the occasion of the Feast of Our Lady of Guadalupe. 12th December 2015.

[23] Morning Meditation in the Chapel of the Domus Sanctae Marthae. 18th December 2014.

[24] Vespers and Te Deum. 31st December 2013.

[25] *The Name of God is Mercy*, p.78.

[26] Wednesday audience catechesis. 16th September 2015.

[27] Morning Meditation in the Chapel of the Domus Sanctae Marthae. 17th December 2013.

[28] Morning Meditation in the Chapel of the Domus Sanctae Marthae. 17th March 2016.

[29] Morning Meditation in the Chapel of the Domus Sanctae Marthae. 25th March 2014.

[30] Morning Meditation in the Chapel of the Domus Sanctae Marthae. 4th April 2016.

[31] Morning Meditation in the Chapel of the Domus Sanctae Marthae. 18th December 2014.

[32] Angelus address. 15th December 2013.

[33] Pope Benedict XVI. Angelus address. 13th December 2009.

[34] *Evangelii Gaudium.*

[35] Angelus address. 15th December 2013.

[36] Otto Pies SJ, The *Victory of Father Karl*, Victor Gollancz, 1957.

[37] Morning Meditation in the Chapel of the Domus Sanctae Marthae. 17th March 2016.

[38] Message to the President of the Cuban Episcopal Conference on the Occasion of the Day of the Nativity of the Blessed Virgin Mary Feast of the Virgen De La Caridad del Cobre, 2014.

[39] Angelus address. 15th December 2013.

[40] Morning Meditation in the Chapel of the Domus Sanctae Marthae. 2nd December 2013.

[41] Homily during pastoral visit to the parish of St Cyril of Alexandria. 1st December 2013.

[42] Morning Meditation in the Chapel of the Domus Sanctae Marthae. 2nd December 2013.

[43] Morning Meditation in the Chapel of the Domus Sanctae Marthae. 17th December 2013.

[44] Homily during pastoral visit to the parish of St Cyril of Alexandria. 1st December 2013.

[45] Homily at the canonisation of St Maria Guadalupe Garcia Zavala & St Laura Montoya. 13th May 2013.

[46] Morning Meditation in the Chapel of the Domus Sanctae Marthae. 18th December 2014.

[47] Morning Meditation in the Chapel of the Domus Sanctae Marthae. 20th December 2013.

[48] Ibid.

[49] Fr John Zuhlsdorf, The O Antiphons *http://www.wdtprs.com/JTZ/o_antiphons/*

[50] Morning Meditation in the Chapel of the Domus Sanctae Marthae. 23rd December 2013.

88

[51] Ibid.

[52] Ibid.

[53] Ibid.

[54] Morning Meditation in the Chapel of the Domus Sanctae Marthae. 19th December 2013.

[55] Address to the young people of Italian Catholic Action. 20th December 2013.

[56] Morning Meditation in the Chapel of the Domus Sanctae Marthae. 12th December 2013.

[57] Morning Meditation in the Chapel of the Domus Sanctae Marthae. 10th December 2015.

[58] Op cit.

[59] Morning Meditation in the Chapel of the Domus Sanctae Marthae. 2nd December 2014.

[60] Ibid.

[61] Morning Meditation in the Chapel of the Domus Sanctae Marthae. 16th December 2014.

[62] Saint Therese of Lisieux: A Gateway http://www.thereseoflisieux.org/my-blog-about-st-therese/2013/5/3/pope-francis-and-saint-therese-of-lisieux-to-depend-solely-o.html#.V1NkkFeJo0o

[63] Midnight Mass. Solemnity of the Nativity of the Lord. 24th December 2013.

[64] Eugenio Scalfari, "The Pope: how the Church will change" http://www.repubblica.it/cultura/2013/10/01/news pope_s_conversation_with_scalfari_english-67643118/

[65] John L Allen, "What's really miraculous about Pope Francis?" http://www.cruxnow.com/church/2015/03/07/whats-really-miraculous-about-pope-francis/

[66] Encyclical letter Lumen Fidei.

[67] Address to pilgrims from Bavaria for the presentation of the gift of the Christmas tree. 13th December 2013.

[68] Address to pilgrims from Verona and Catanzaro for the presentation of the gift of the Christmas tree. 19th December 2014.

[69] Midnight Mass. Solemnity of the Nativity of the Lord. 24th December 2013.

[70] Angelus address. 9th February 2014.

[71] Homily for the solemnity of the Epiphany. 6th January 2016 http://en.radiovaticana.va/news/2016/01/06/pope_francis_church_doesn't_shine_with_its_own_light/1199171

[72] Angelus address, Solemnity of the Epiphany of the Lord. 6th January 2016.